In the TOOLSHED

by Pearl Markovics

Consultant:
Beth Gambro
Reading Specialist
Yorkville, Illinois

Contents

BEARPORT
PUBLISHING

New York, New York

In the Toolshed

Look around.

What do you see?

I see nails in the toolshed.

What do you see?

I see gloves in the toolshed.

What do you see?

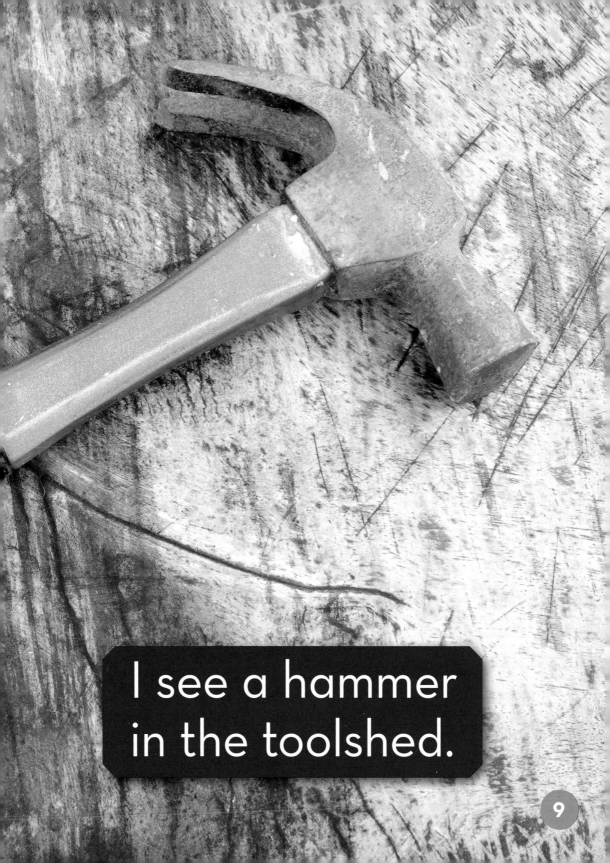

I see a hammer in the toolshed.

What do you see?

I see shovels in the toolshed.

What do you see?

I see a rake in the toolshed.

Look closely!

What do you see
in the toolshed?

Key Words

gloves

hammer

nails

rake

shovels

Index

About the Author

Pearl Markovics grew up on a small farm in New York. She enjoys collecting and using tools of every kind.

Teaching Tips

Before Reading

✔ Guide readers on a "picture walk" through the text by asking them to name the things shown.

✔ Discuss book structure by showing children where text will appear consistently on pages.

✔ Highlight the supportive pattern of the book. Note the consistent number of sentences found on each page.

During Reading

✔ Encourage readers to "read with your finger" and point to each word as it is read. Stop periodically to ask children to point to a specific word in the text.

✔ Reading strategies: When encountering unknown words, prompt readers with encouraging cues such as:

- **Does that word look like a word you already know?**
- **Check the picture.**

After Reading

✔ Write the key words on index cards.

- **Have readers match them to pictures in the book.**
- **Have children sort words by category (words that include the letter *a*, for example).**

✔ Ask readers to identify their favorite page in the book. Have them read that page aloud.

✔ Ask children to write their own sentences. Encourage them to use the same pattern found in the book as a model for their writing.

Credits: Cover, © thieury/Shutterstock; 2–3, © Kuriputosu/iStock; 4–5, © SutidaS/iStock; 6–7, © Kelsey Olson/Shutterstock; 8–9, © Jiggo_thekop/iStock; 10–11, © Jinning Li/Shutterstock; 12–13, © Plamen Galabov/Shutterstock; 14–15, © Pikselstock/Shutterstock; 16T (L to R), © Kelsey Olson/Shutterstock and © Jiggo_thekop/iStock; 16B (L to R), © SutidaS/iStock, © Plamen Galabov/Shutterstock, and © Jinning Li/Shutterstock.

Publisher: Kenn Goin   **Senior Editor**: Joyce Tavolacci   **Creative Director**: Spencer Brinker   **Photo Researcher**: Thomas Persano

Library of Congress Cataloging-in-Publication Data in process at the time of publication (2019)
Library of Congress Control Number: 2018047570
ISBN-13: 978-1-64280-207-8 / ISBN: 978-1-64280-380-8 (paperback)